André Leblanc

For the Price of a Song

A Century of Child Labour 1850-1950

Translated by Jane Macaulay

Smith, Bonappétit & Son

Montreal, Toronto

Legal Deposit: 3rd quarter 2006
Bibliothèque et Archives nationales du Québec
Library and Archives Canada

Cataloguing in Publication Data (Canada)

Leblanc, André, 1940-
For the price of a song: A century of child labour, 1850-1950 / André
Leblanc; translated from the French by Jane Macaulay.

(Our history in pictures)
Translation of: L'envers de la chanson.
For ages 8-12.

ISBN-10 : 1-897118-17-1
ISBN-13 : 978-1-897118-17-7

1. Child labour—Canada—History—19th century—Pictorial works—
Juvenile literature. 2. Child labour—Canada—History—20th century—
Pictorial works—Juvenile literature. I. Macaulay, Jane II. Title. III. Series.

HD6250.C32L4314 2006   j331.3'1'09710222   C2005-906867-1

The publisher wishes to acknowledge the support of
the Canada Council for the Arts for this publishing
program. We are also thankful to the SODEC.

The translation of this book was made possible
through the financial support of the Canada Council
for the Arts and Heritage Canada through the
Book Publishing Industry Development Program.

Government of Québec—Tax credit for book
publishing— Administered by SODEC

For the Price of a Song
A Century of Child Labour 1850–1950
Editor: Catherine Germain
Design and photo colouring: Andrée Lauzon
Copy Editor: Marie Lauzon

Distributor for Canada:
Fraser Direct
100 Armstrong Avenue
Georgetown, ON L7G 5S4

Printed in Canada by Groupe Quadriscan.

I learned the songs of my childhood at my parents'
and grandparents' knees. Much later, I discovered
how hard they had worked as children and came to
understand that there are two sides to every song.

A. L.

"If I had wings like Noah's dove, I'd fly across the
water to the one I love…"

Once long ago…

…When my father was seven, my grand-father took him out of school. It was in the year 1914. The family was poor and everyone had to pitch in to help with the farm work, even the very youngest.

My father had barely learned to count or say his alphabet. But there would be no more schoolbooks for him! He had to start working in the fields, leading the horse that ploughed the earth, picking berries that stained his hands, digging up potatoes covered with dirt and hauling heavy, round cabbages.

"Oats, peas, beans and barley grow… Do you or I or anyone know, how oats, peas, beans and barley grow?"

"Oh the fox went out on a chilly night, prayed for the moon to give him light, for he'd many a mile to go that night before he reached the town-o…"

If ever I asked my father how old he was when he started to work, he would always say:
"I was fourteen."
"So what were you doing between seven and fourteen, since you weren't going to school anymore?"
"I was on the farm, of course."
"But what were you doing on the farm?"
"Oh well, I was helping out…"

"Here we go gathering nuts in May… on a cold and frosty morning."

"To help out" was a real action verb. It covered all the tasks my father had to do, even though he would never learn to read or write the words for them.
Instead, he learned to sow, plant, weed, pick, gather and pull up crops; to feed, care for and lead the farm animals. That's what helping out meant.
It meant work — hard work, without pay!

"Speed bonny boat like a bird on the wing,
'Onward!' the sailors cry..."

My father's situation was far from rare. Children were so useful on farms that, until 1925, Canada brought thousands of orphans over from England.★ Almost as soon as these girls and boys got off the ships that brought them here, they were sent to farms, especially in the Canadian West, where they were taught to work on the land.

★ In this period, Great Britain attempted to reduce poverty in the cities by encouraging benevolent societies to send abandoned children overseas. Around 1900, the Barnardo Foundation alone transferred 28,000 children to Canada. For each child, Canada paid a small amount of money.

"There's a hole in my bucket, dear Eliza, dear Eliza.
There's a hole in my bucket, dear Eliza, a hole."

In the country, children were responsible for many everyday tasks, from the simplest to the most complicated. This was part of an age-old tradition, dating back to the very beginnings of agriculture.

Children fed the farm animals – horses, cows, calves and chickens. There was no indoor plumbing, and water had to be fetched at an outdoor well and hauled in buckets. Cows had to be milked. Manure had to be shovelled. And wood had to be carried inside to keep the fire burning in the wood stove.

The youngest children imitated the older ones, and the older ones looked after the youngest.

"The water is wide, I can't cross over, neither have I wings to fly.
Give me a boat that will carry two, and both shall row my love and I."

Children did all kinds of jobs in every season.

In summer, young boys were often seen selling water by the roadside, near country train stations, or along railroads.

In winter, boys could also find work cutting ice on the frozen rivers. Their wool mittens would become stiff as they hacked at the hard ice with heavy iron bars. At the time, there were no refrigerators. People kept perishable food in iceboxes, which were like insulated cupboards, cooled by large blocks of ice.

Then, when spring was on the way, boys would lend a hand to the men who broke up ice jams on the river.

In fishing villages, children lived by the rhythms of the tide. They had to rise before dawn and were often still at work when night fell.

From sea to sea, children were actively involved in fishing. In British Columbia, they had to haul up nets filled with thrashing salmon. In Newfoundland, they had to help catch the cod and then clean, wash and salt it. The salted fish was laid out to dry on the wharfs for several weeks, as a way of preserving it.

Fishing was dangerous work. The salt made your skin crack and the cold water numbed your hands and feet. You had to watch your step on the slippery wharfs, keep an eye out for any hooks lying about and avoid tipping overloaded wheelbarrows.

"I'se the boy who builds the boat and I'se the boy that sails her, I'se the boy that catches the fish and takes them home to Liza."

Working underground was even more difficult. My grandfather would jokingly threaten us: "If you scamps don't behave, I'll send you to the mines!"

In the early 1800s, boys aged eight to fourteen went down mine shafts to work in the galleries. They led the blind ponies that pulled the carts. They operated the ventilation doors. They helped the miners extract and load the coal. And deep inside the earth, they had to deal constantly with darkness, rats and fear.

Accidents were frequent. In one of them, more than 125 men and children perished when gas exploded in the Springhill Mine, Nova Scotia, in February 1891.

"The day still comes and the sun still shines, but it's dark as the grave in the Cumberland Mine..."

In the copper mines around Bolton, in the Eastern Townships, in Quebec, girls were also put to work. Along with boys, they carried out surface jobs such as separating ore from rock in the sorting sheds.

These children – some of them barely over twelve – worked ten hours a day.

"Freight train, freight train, run so fast... Please don't tell what train I'm on; they won't know what route I've gone..."

When my maternal grandmother was eight, she moved with her family to Lowell, an industrial town in northern Massachusetts. It was the year 1887.★

Day in and day out, she helped her mother, cleaning, cooking and doing laundry for wealthy people. She never went to school and she never learned to read or write.

★ Around this time, a million French Canadians left Quebec for New England with hopes of improving their lot.

"This is the way we bake our bread...
This is the way we bake our bread,
so early Saturday morning."

When my grandmother turned 11, she followed her brothers' and sisters' example and found a job in the cotton mills.★

"Back then, you worked thirteen hours a day," she would tell me. "The factory bell rang at four-thirty in the morning and, by five, you were at work. When all the weaving machines were running, the noise was terrible. It would grow louder and louder. But after a while you got used to it – it was as if you were deaf. We were covered in cotton dust. The machines gave off so much heat, it was unbearable, even in winter."

★ The youngest children had the job of climbing up on the machines to reattach broken threads and replace empty bobbins.

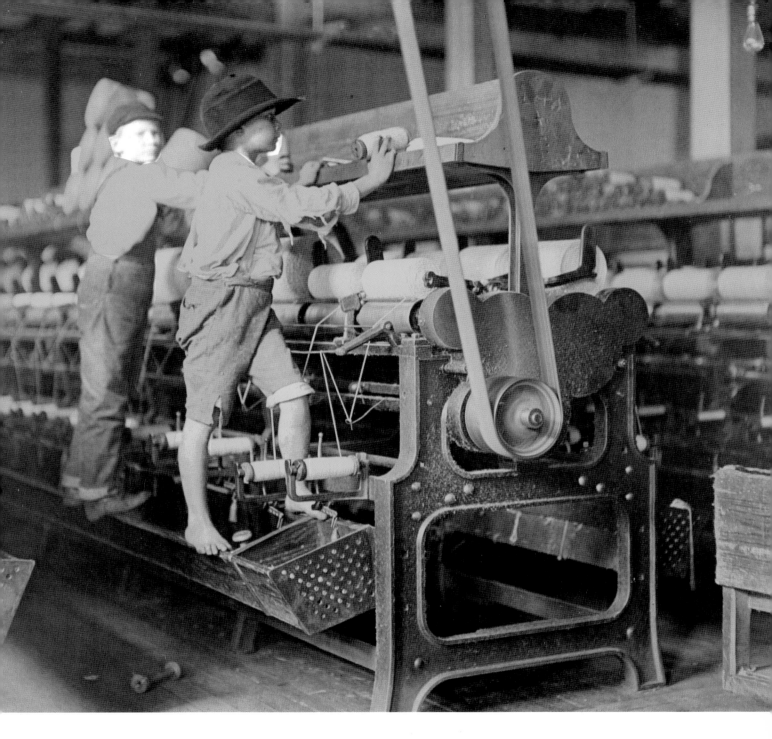

"Wind the bobbin, wind the bobbin. Pull, pull, tap, tap, tap..."

In 1913, the work week in Canadian cotton mills was fixed at just 55 hours, since these factories employed many children and working conditions in them were considered to be difficult and depressing. However, in many other sectors, children continued to work for up to 72 hours a week.

"After the foremen locked the doors, there was no let-up," my grandmother said. "Often, we had to eat our lunch while the machines were still running. There was danger all around. If you were drowsy or let your thoughts wander, you could have an accident. I saw people lose fingers, arms – even their lives. It was really tough!"

But, on a few rare occasions, the children had a little break – the time for a photograph to be taken – and a sunbeam might suddenly stream through a window.

"Alouette, gentille alouette, alouette
je te plumerai…"

★ Jobs change with the times. In 1910, you could find work pressing records that would be played on the recently invented gramophone. Or you might be paid to starch detachable collars and cuffs for shirts. These jobs have now disappeared.

Everywhere, children were at work, hired as apprentices for all kinds of labour. They could be found in cigar factories, tailors' workshops, laundries, shoemaker's shops and stores. They were employed in bakeries, match factories and even slaughterhouses.★ Boys could begin to work at the age of 12, while the legal age for girls was 14. But very often employers did not bother about these rules and government inspectors turned a blind eye.

"Again I am a bachelor, I live with my son; we work at the weaver's trade…"

Until 1920, the average worker's wages were not enough to meet the basic needs of a family. Children were sent to work out of necessity. They earned half as much as women and four times less than men. A child was paid four dollars a week, or six cents an hour.

"You have to understand, back then, we didn't have our pictures taken very often. So it would be really unusual to be photographed at work!" That is what my grandmother had to say about photographers. And it is true that children were rarely photographed at their tasks.

When a photographer ventured into a place of work, he usually just assembled everyone for a group portrait. Then he would shout, "Alright! Nobody move! Watch the birdie!" ★ The photograph would show the group looking somewhat like a family, with well-behaved children surrounded by adults. Everyone posed stiffly, wearing a proud, serious expression.

"Bluebird, bluebird through my window... Bluebird, bluebird through my window, Johnny I am tired..."

★ To make sure that everyone was looking at the camera, some photographers would hold up a little mechanical bird that twittered when he took the picture.

★ Such a fine equalled
two hours of wages.

One thing, however, was never captured by the camera, and that was the harshness of the rules enforced in some places of work.

In the 1880s, in Montreal, the Royal Commission on the Relation of Labour and Capital heard the testimony of a worker concerning the appalling conditions that employees faced at his factory. "If a child does something – for example, looking from side to side, or talking – the foreman says, 'I'm going to fine you 10 cents.'★ And if the child does the same thing two or three more times, well, the foreman takes a stick or a piece of wood and beats the youngster with it."

"See-saw, Margery Daw, Jacky shall have a new master. He will have but a penny a day because he can't work any faster."

Other children worked directly for their family. Whenever my sisters and I complained about school, our grandmother would tell us about the children who had the job of gathering coal. Between about 1900 and 1930, these children, girls for the most part, could be seen picking up lumps of coal that had fallen from freight cars along the train tracks. This coal was the only fuel their families had to heat their homes and cook their food.
If the little girls gathered more than the family needed, they would sell it to other people in the neighbourhood.

"Red light, green light 'round the town, I found a penny on the ground. Met a friend I never knowed, walking down old rocky road."

"… If your feet are nimble and light,
you can get there by candle-light."

In the early 1900s, young messenger boys dressed in the colours of
the new telegraph companies could be seen on city streets, dashing
here and there on bicycles to deliver telegrams. The telegram was
an exciting invention at the time. Now people could send messages
in a special code over long distances by electric wire.

From early morning to late evening, the streets echoed with the
cries of newspaper boys. This was the dawn of the communication
era, long before the invention of television and the Internet.

As the factories became more and more automated, things began
to improve; but that didn't mean child labour disappeared, as
families still struggled to get by. But some were beginning to see
hope for a better life.

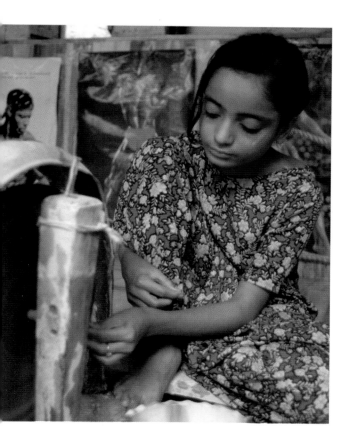

But the story doesn't end here!

Child labour has now been abolished in the "wealthy" countries of North America and Europe, but elsewhere in the world little has changed.

Today, very young girls and boys still work every day. Some polish precious stones or weave carpets. Others carry bricks or pick up garbage, and still others break stones or put matches in boxes. Nearly 300 million of the world's children work, and three quarters of them do so in conditions that are difficult and often dangerous.

The rest of the world's children are like you – they are "lucky enough to go to school." That's what my father and grandmother used to say to me! They knew that giving children an education meant giving them a chance to gain more freedom as men and women.

"But whoever treasures freedom, like the swallow, has learned to fly."

PHOTO CRÉDITS

ANQ   Archives nationales du Québec
AO   Archives of Ontario
LAC   Library and Archives Canada
EFM   Écomusée du fier monde
MCM   McCord Museum
CSTM   Canada Science and Technology Museum
NARA   US National Archives and Records Administration
NSM   Nova Scotia Museum
SHSH   Société historique de Saint-Henri
ILO   International Labor Organization

Cover photographs: Anonymous, Young girl with a bag of coal, Toronto, Ontario, ca. 1900, Kelso Coll., LAC / PA-118224; Lewis W. Hine, Children had to climb up to the spinning frame, Bibb Mill No. 1, Macon, Georgia (USA), 1909. NARA / ARC 523148 (detail)

Inner cover: François Fleury, Harvesting potatoes, Saint-Lambert (South Shore of Montreal), 1943, ANQ / E6.S7.P16121

Page 3: Donat-C. Noiseux, Sifting grain, Quebec, 1942, ANQ / E6.S7.P9833 (detail)

Pages 4 and 5: Anonymous, Children gathering potatoes in Prince Edward Island, ca. 1921, LAC / PA-043964

Pages 6 and 7: Reuben Sallows, Harvesters crossing a field, Ontario (n.d.), 1906, AO / C 223-4-0-0-14

Pages 8 and 9: E.L. Désilets, Pulling up flax, Caplan, Gaspé Peninsula (Quebec), 1948, ANQ / E6.S7.P67073

Pages 10 and 11: Anonymous, A boy plowing at Dr. Barnardo's Industrial Farm, Russell, Manitoba, ca. 1900, LAC / PA-117285

Pages 12 and 13: Anonymous, Some children in the Raymond family coming back from milking the cows, Henryville (Quebec), 1928, private collection; Ken H. Hand, Boy feeding a calf, Loon Lake, Saskatchewan, 1951, CSTM / CN 001745

Pages 14 and 15: Anonymous, Water boy, Val-Jalbert (Quebec), ca. 1925, CSTM / CN 000683; Charles H. Millar, Ice jam on canal in front of old mill (or Ice cutting), Drummondville (Quebec), ca. 1895, MCM/ MP-1974.133.11

Pages 16 and 17: Dorothy Bowles, Drying fish, Gaultors (Newfoundland), 1935, NSM / F94.46.57; Anonymous, Salmon in drag seine net on the Nimpkish River, British Colombia, ca. 1930, LAC / PA-205827

Pages 18 and 19: Anonymous, The coal miners, Canada, n.d., 1915, LAC / C-046320

Pages 20 and 21: Anonymous, A 14-year-old coal miner, Manitoba, ca. 1912, in the Report on Neglected Children by F. J. Billiarde, LAC / C-030945; William Notman, Separating the ore from the rock, Huntington Copper Mine, Bolton (Quebec), 1867, MCM / N-0000.94.58

Pages 22 and 23: Attr. to James or May Ballantyne, Young girl in a kitchen at 54 Main Street, Ottawa (Ontario), 1907, LAC / PA-133676

Pages 24 and 25: Lewis W. Hine, One of the little spinners working, Lancaster Cotton Mills, South Carolina (USA), 1908, NARA / ARC-523122 (detail); Lewis W. Hine, Children had to climb up to the spinning frame, Bibb Mill No. 1, Macon, Georgia (USA), 1909, NARA / ARC-523148 (detail)

Pages 26 and 27: Anonymous, Children working in the cotton mills, Montreal (Quebec), n.d., EFM / 2003.335

Pages 28 and 29: Anonymous, Interior of the Berliner Gramophone Company, Montreal (Quebec), 1910, MCM / MP-1982.69.1; N. M. Hinshelwood, Women starching collars and cuffs, M.T.S., Montreal (Quebec), n.d., ca. 1901, MCM / MP-1985.31.181

Pages 30 and 31: Anonymous, Group of workers at the Lecavalier and Riel slaughterhouses, Saint-Henri (Quebec), ca. 1890, SHSH / #142-ph-42(D); Anonymous, Le Pain Suprême Bakery, Brewster St., Saint-Henri (Quebec), 1915, SHSH / #74-ph-1

Pages 32 and 33: Anonymous, Match factory. Girls packaging matches, Saint-Casimir-de-Portneuf (Quebec), 1910, ANQ / P711.PSE-495.2; Anonymous, Printing shop. The magazine L'Action Catholique, Sainte-Anne (Quebec), 1908-1910, ANQ / P428.S3.D2P1

Pages 34 and 35: Anonymous, Girls collecting coal by the train tracks, Toronto (Ontario), ca. 1900, Kelso Coll., LAC / PA-181961

Pages 36 and 37: Anonymous, Messenger service. Office of the G.N.W. Telegraph Co., Montreal (Quebec), 1900, LAC / PA-117883; Anonymous, Newsboy selling papers on street, Montreal (Quebec), ca. 1905, MCM / MP-0000.586.112

Pages 38 and 39: J.M. Derrien, Young brick carriers, Madagascar, n.d., ILO / c0041; A. Khemka, Gem polishing industry, Jaipur (India), 2000, ILO / c1552

Page 40: Richard S. Cassels, Boy carrying water buckets on yoke, Cacouna (Quebec), 1898, LAC / PA-123289